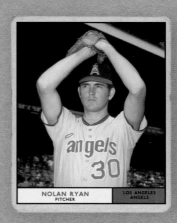

NOLAN RYAN
PITCHER

LOS ANGELES
ANGELS

TROY GLAUS
THIRD BASEMAN

LOS ANGELES
ANGELS

THE STORY OF THE LOS ANGELES ANGELS

Published by Creative Education
P.O. Box 227, Mankato, Minnesota 56002
Creative Education is an imprint of The Creative Company
www.thecreativecompany.us

Design and production by Blue Design
Art direction by Rita Marshall
Printed by Corporate Graphics in the United States of America

Photographs by Getty Images (Doug Benc, Scott Boehm, P Brouillet, Ralph Crane/Time & Life Pictures, Jonathan Daniel, Diamond Images, Stephen Dunn, Don Emmert/AFP, Focus on Sport, Otto Greule Jr, Leon Halip, Scott Halleran, Jeff Haynes/AFP, David Hofmann, Harry How, Kurt Hutton/Picture Post, Walter Iooss Jr./Sports Illustrated, Jed Jacobsohn, V.J. Lovero, Ronald Martinez, Rich Pilling/MLB Photos, Mike Powell, Louis Requena/MLB Photos), National Baseball Hall of Fame Library, Cooperstown, N.Y.

Library of Congress Cataloging-in-Publication Data

Gilbert, Sara.
The story of the Los Angeles Angels of Anaheim / by Sara Gilbert.
p. cm. — (Baseball: the great American game)
Includes index.
Summary: The history of the Los Angeles Angels of Anaheim professional baseball team from its inaugural 1961 season to today, spotlighting the team's greatest players and most memorable moments.
ISBN 978-1-60818-044-8
1. Los Angeles Angels of Anaheim (Baseball team)—History—Juvenile literature. I. Title. II. Series.

GV875.L6G55 2011
796.357'640979496—dc22   2010024401

CPSIA: 110310 PO1381

First Edition
9 8 7 6 5 4 3 2 1

Page 3: First baseman Rod Carew
Page 4: Center fielder Torii Hunter

BASEBALL: THE GREAT AMERICAN GAME

THE STORY OF THE LOS ANGELES ANGELS

Sara Gilbert

CREATIVE EDUCATION

CONTENTS

CHAPTERS

A Star-Studded Start 6

Changing Tides 15

Fallen Angels 22

Angels Take Flight 33

Happy Halos 37

AROUND THE HORN

The Singing Cowboy 12

Playing in the Postseason 20

What's in a Name? 24

Monkey Business 31

A Major First for Minorities 38

Angels among Them 43

ALL-TIME ANGELS

P — Nolan Ryan 8

C — Buck Rodgers 13

1B — Wally Joyner 14

2B — Bobby Grich 18

3B — Troy Glaus 23

SS — Jim Fregosi 28

LF — Brian Downing 30

CF — Darin Erstad 35

RF — Garret Anderson 39

M — Mike Scioscia 40

Index 48

STAR-STUDDED START

The German farmers and winemakers who founded the city of Anaheim in 1857 named it after the picturesque Santa Ana River, which tumbles through the hills near the original site of the city. They paired "Ana" with *heim*, the German word for "home," to designate the new town as their home by the river. At first, Anaheim was settled by a relatively small population. Today, it is the 10th-largest city in California, home to a diverse population of almost 350,000. That figure doesn't include the thousands of visitors who come to Anaheim and the greater Los Angeles area each year to enjoy its many attractions, from theme parks such as Disneyland and Universal Studios to the exquisite landscape, including beautiful white beaches and rugged mountains.

Many visitors to the region also make a stop at Angel Stadium of Anaheim, the home of the city's Major League Baseball franchise, the Los Angeles Angels of Anaheim. The original Angels began their existence in the nearby urban center of Los Angeles in 1960, when

Home to the biggest movie studios and many artists of all kinds, Los Angeles is sometimes called the "Entertainment Capital of the World."

PITCHER · NOLAN RYAN

On August 20, 1974, Angels pitcher Nolan Ryan landed in *The Guinness Book of World Records* when his fastball was clocked at 100.9 miles per hour. That blazing pitch was already the infamous calling card of "The Ryan Express," who tossed the first four of his seven career no-hitters with the Angels. Ryan went on to intimidate big-league batters for 27 seasons, striking out an incredible 1,176 different players on his way to setting several records—including 5,714 total "K's," the all-time major-league record. Ryan was elected to the Baseball Hall of Fame in his first year of eligibility.

NOLAN RYAN
PITCHER

LOS ANGELES
ANGELS

STATS

Angels seasons: 1972–79

Height: 6-foot-2

Weight: 170

- **5,714 career strikeouts**

- **7 career no-hitters**

- **8-time All-Star**

- **Baseball Hall of Fame inductee (1999)**

entertainer Gene Autry was awarded ownership of an American League (AL) expansion team that he named the Angels.

Autry's Angels, led by veteran pitcher Eli Grba and 19-year-old shortstop Jim Fregosi, played their first game on April 11, 1961. Back-to-back home runs by first baseman Ted Kluszewski and outfielder Bob Cerv in the first inning propelled the Angels to a 7–2 victory over the Baltimore Orioles. Kluszewski's powerful bat and Grba's strong pitching helped Los Angeles cobble together a 70–91 record during its first year. Although that put the team 8th among the 10 AL teams, it also set a major-league record for the best winning percentage by a first-year team. The next season was even better, as the Angels finished with a winning record—in third place and only 10 games out of the playoffs.

As the '60s went on, the Angels' success increased, fueled in part by the lively fastball of right-handed pitcher Dean Chance. In 1964, Chance accounted for 20 of the team's 82 wins and won the AL Cy Young Award at the age of 23—making him, at the time, the youngest player ever to be honored as the league's best pitcher. That same year, Fregosi hit his stride. The 22-year-old batted .277 with 18 homers and 72 runs batted in (RBI) and made the first of his 6 appearances in the All-Star Game.

The expansion "Halos" played their first nine seasons under the guidance of manager Bill Rigney (right).

BILL RIGNEY

Thanks to these efforts, the Angels posted their second winning record.

In 1966, the Angels moved out of Los Angeles and into suburban Anaheim, settling into the brand-new Anaheim Stadium. With a new park and a new name—the team was now known as the California Angels—the team's fan base multiplied. Attendance at home games jumped from 566,727 in 1965 to 1.4 million in 1966.

The team posted an 80–82 record that year and improved to 84–77 in 1967. Still, the Angels remained far from postseason contention. In 1968, they finished 36 games behind the league-leading Detroit Tigers, and in 1969, they ended 26 games out. The 1970 Angels played much better as a whole, posting an 86–76 record—their best since 1962. It was a big year for left fielder Alex Johnson, who laid claim to the first league batting title in team history with a .329 average. He barely edged out Boston Red Sox slugger Carl Yastrzemski by getting two hits on the last day of the season. "This is my biggest individual achievement," said Johnson. "The silver bat will be an elegant addition to my trophy case."

California native Jim Fregosi did a little bit of everything for the Angels; by the time he left Los Angeles in 1971, he had helped turn 818 double plays.

THE SINGING COWBOY

Gene Autry became famous for singing songs from atop his constant companion, Champion the Wonder Horse. During his legendary career in show business, Autry wrote more than 200 songs, appeared in almost 100 movies, and produced his own TV series. By the time "The Singing Cowboy" retired in the early 1960s, he had amassed a considerable fortune—and decided to invest some of it in the Los Angeles Angels when the team joined the AL in 1961. Autry was the Angels' sole owner for more than 30 years and became almost as recognizable on the baseball diamond as he had been on the silver screen. It didn't hurt that he continued to wear the trademark white cowboy hat that had defined his presence in film and on TV. Autry, who sold part of the franchise to the Walt Disney Company in 1997, died at the age of 91 a year later and never got to see the team he helped build win a World Series. But when the Angels finally captured the crown in 2002, the team's longtime owner was undoubtedly present in spirit. As the Angels celebrated their Game 7 victory, outfielder Tim Salmon waved a white cowboy hat in the air in Autry's honor.

ANGELS

CATCHER · BUCK RODGERS

Buck Rodgers was just 22 when he played his first game for the Los Angeles Angels in 1961. He spent the next nine years crouching behind the plate in an Angels uniform, compiling an impressive .988 fielding average. Rodgers went on to serve as skipper for the Milwaukee Brewers and Montreal Expos before returning to the Angels in 1991, putting together a career record of 784–774. In 1992, he missed almost 90 games after being injured when the Angels' bus was involved in an accident; his injuries had a lasting and detrimental effect on his ability to lead, resulting in his dismissal in May 1994.

BUCK RODGERS
CATCHER

LOS ANGELES
ANGELS

STATS

Angels seasons: 1961–69 (as player), 1991–94 (as manager)

Height: 6-foot-2

Weight: 190

- 31 career HR

- .988 career fielding average

- 4,750 career putouts

- 1987 NL Manager of the Year award

ANGELS

FIRST BASEMAN · WALLY JOYNER

Wally Joyner took over first base for the Angels in 1986 and promptly became a favorite among California fans, whose votes earned him a starting spot in the All-Star Game as a rookie. A year later, Joyner slammed 34 home runs and earned team Most Valuable Player (MVP) honors. He went on to hit more than 200 homers during his illustrious career, which spanned 16 years and 4 teams. Joyner returned to the Angels for his final big-league season in 2001. A religious man, Joyner went on to appear in movies marketed to members of The Church of Jesus Christ of Latter-Day Saints.

STATS

Angels seasons: 1986–91, 2001

Height: 6-foot-2

Weight: 185

• 204 career HR

• 1,106 career RBI

• .289 career BA

• 1986 All-Star

WALLY JOYNER
FIRST BASEMAN

LOS ANGELES
ANGELS

CHANGING TIDES

Meanwhile, the Angels' trophy case was still bare after a decade of play. In an effort to start filling it, the team traded fan favorite Fregosi to the New York Mets in 1971 for a young pitcher with a wild arm and a wicked fastball—Nolan Ryan. The next year, Ryan struck out 383 batters and threw the first 2 of his 7 career no-hitters. "I honestly never felt I was the type of pitcher to pitch a no-hitter," Ryan said after the first, on May 15, 1973, against the Kansas City Royals. Two months later, he tossed his second "no-no" in a game against the Tigers.

Despite Ryan's dominance, the Angels struggled to climb above .500 in the early 1970s. It wasn't until 1978 that they posted another winning record, finishing in a tie for second in the AL Western Division (the league had been split into two divisions in 1969). Still, almost two decades into their existence, the Angels had yet to experience postseason play.

That finally changed in 1979, when former star Jim Fregosi began his first full season as team manager. The Angels led the league in runs scored (866) on their way to an 88–74 record and first-ever AL West championship. Veterans such as

first baseman Rod Carew, second

baseman Bobby Grich, and right

fielder Dan Ford each had fine seasons, and Ryan won 16 games, but it

was stocky slugger Don Baylor who had the most spectacular season of

all. The left fielder finished with a .296 average, a league-leading 139 RBI,

and the AL MVP award. "Every day I went to the park, I knew I'd get

two or three hits and some RBI," Baylor explained. "I got off to a good

start and was in the right frame of mind."

The Angels then squared off against the Baltimore Orioles in the

AL Championship Series (ALCS). During each of the first three games,

California took an early lead. But an extra-inning home run by Orioles

pinch hitter John Lowenstein ended Game 1 in Baltimore's favor, and

Game 2 again went to the Orioles. The Angels got their only win of the

series in Game 3 before being blanked 8–0 in Game 4.

That first taste of postseason play whetted the Angels' appetite

for more. But Ryan, a free agent after the 1979 season, jumped at the

chance to return to his home state of Texas and play for the Houston

NOLAN RYAN

SECOND BASEMAN · BOBBY GRICH

Although he started his career as a shortstop, Bobby Grich made a name for himself as a second baseman. Twice, the lanky infielder set team single-season records for fielding— including when he finished the 1985 season with just two errors and a .997 fielding percentage. The most memorable of Grich's 224 home runs was his last: He hit a two-run dinger in the sixth inning of Game 5 of the 1986 ALCS that helped send the game into extra innings. But the Boston Red Sox came back to win that game, as well as the next two. Grich retired after the series ended.

STATS

Angels seasons: 1977–86

Height: 6-foot-2

Weight: 180

- **6-time All-Star**

- **4-time Gold Glove winner**

- **224 career HR**

- **864 career RBI**

BOBBY GRICH
SECOND BASEMAN

LOS ANGELES
ANGELS

Astros. Without its star hurler, the team stumbled. Baylor's offensive production was hampered by injuries, and although the sweet-swinging Carew posted a terrific .331 batting average, the 1980 Angels finished a disappointing 65–95. The 1981 season, which was shortened by a players' strike, was only slightly more successful. After finishing at or near the bottom of the division for two consecutive seasons, the Angels could only hope that there was nowhere to go but up.

The 1982 Angels team was, as Grich put it, "made up of veterans with sore muscles, with tired arms, with drained emotions." But those depleted players got a lift from the addition of another veteran who still had some highlights left in him: Reggie Jackson, a power-hitting right fielder who had been slamming balls out of stadiums around the league since 1967. Although he joined the Angels in the twilight of his career, he still led the league with 39 home runs in 1982.

With Jackson in the lineup, Baylor healthy again, and catcher Brian Downing blossoming offensively, the Angels racked up 93 wins and found themselves back in the ALCS, this time against the Milwaukee Brewers. California charged into the series, winning Game 1 behind

PLAYING IN THE POSTSEASON

The scoreboard in Anaheim Stadium often flashed with three simple words in 1979: "Yes We Can." And California could. After 18 years, the Angels finally played well enough to win their division and make it to the playoffs. The leader of the charge was Don Baylor, the powerful left fielder who earned AL MVP honors after hitting .296 with 36 home runs and 139 RBI. But he had help. Second baseman Bobby Grich and right fielder Dan Ford each posted 101 RBI; Nolan Ryan earned 16 wins, 1 of which was a single inning away from becoming his fifth no-hitter as an Angels pitcher; and first baseman Rod Carew posted a .318 average in his first season with the team. "The biggest thing we had to overcome was that we had never won a division," said Jim Fregosi, the former star shortstop who had returned as manager midway through the previous season. "No matter how good the talent was, there seemed to be a black cloud hanging over the team. Overcoming that was special to me." Although the Angels fell to a superior Baltimore Orioles team in the playoffs, the postseason monkey was finally off their backs.

DON BAYLOR

pitcher Tommy John, who allowed only seven hits in a complete-game effort. When the Angels won Game 2 to take a two-games-to-none lead over the Brewers, it looked like the "Halos" were on their way to the World Series. Then play shifted to Milwaukee's County Stadium, where the tide turned. The Brewers won Games 3 and 4, forcing a deciding Game 5 in Milwaukee. With the Angels up 3–2 in the seventh inning, Brewers first baseman Cecil Cooper drove in two runs with a base hit. The Angels couldn't come back, losing both the game and the series. Still, Angels center fielder Fred Lynn, who compiled a .611 batting average throughout the five games, was honored as the MVP of the ALCS.

FALLEN ANGELS

he dejected Angels took their time recovering from the disappointment of 1982. The only major highlight of the 70–92 season that followed was Jackson's 500th career home run. In 1984, 15-game winner Mike Witt threw a perfect game and helped the team finish just 3 victories shy of the AL West title. In 1985, the Angels were contenders up to the

THIRD BASEMAN · TROY GLAUS

The Angels showed great foresight when they selected Troy Glaus in the 1997 amateur draft. The powerful young infielder got his first hit in his first game and his first home run two weeks later. He swatted almost 200 more long balls in an Angels uniform, including 7 during the team's successful 2002 postseason campaign. It was Glaus's double in Game 6 of the World Series that scored the winning runs and forced a seventh game. In 2003, he became the first member of the Angels since 1986 to be voted an All-Star Game starter.

STATS

Angels seasons: 1998–2004

Height: 6-foot-5

Weight: 240

- **4-time All-Star**
- **2002 World Series MVP**
- **950 career RBI**
- **320 career HR**

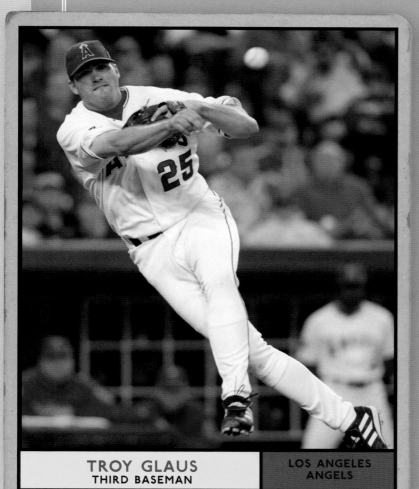

TROY GLAUS
THIRD BASEMAN

LOS ANGELES
ANGELS

WHAT'S IN A NAME?

Since their inception in 1961, the Angels have been known by a number of official names. Originally, when they played in Wrigley Field and Dodger Stadium, both in Los Angeles, they were the Los Angeles Angels. Then, when they moved to the suburb of Anaheim in 1966, they became known more broadly as the California Angels. And when Anaheim Stadium was completely remodeled prior to the 1997 season, they once again changed names—this time to the Anaheim Angels. But the biggest change came in January 2005, when the team's ownership announced another new name: the Los Angeles Angels of Anaheim. Team executives said the change would help them market the club to the entire Southern California region while still complying with the provision in the team's lease with the now-named Angel Stadium that "Anaheim" be included in the team's name. Unfortunately, the new name spurred a legal dispute with the city of Anaheim, which believed that the change violated the "spirit of the lease." Both a jury and a court of appeals ruled in favor of the team, allowing the name change to stand. Yet to those who love them best, the Angels will always be simply the "Halos."

REGGIE JACKSON

end, with 4 players pounding 20 or more home runs, including Downing (with 20) and Jackson (with 27). Although they faded in September, the Angels finished the season just one win short of the division title.

California had high hopes going into the 1986 season. And when Grich drove the first pitch of the season out of the park, Angels fans started dreaming of a trip to the World Series. The team gave them reason to hope, securing 25 come-from-behind victories at Anaheim Stadium en route to a division-winning 92–70 mark. Pitcher Don Sutton earned his 300th career victory in June, and young first baseman Wally Joyner hit .290 and drove in 100 runs. Even at age 40, Jackson proved he could still muscle the ball out of the park, belting 3 home runs in a single game.

The Angels met the Boston Red Sox in the ALCS and dominated three of the first four games. It looked as if they had the series locked up in Game 5, when they entered the ninth inning with a 5–2 lead. Unfortunately, former Angels star Don Baylor hit a two-run homer for Boston, followed by another two-run shot from outfielder Dave Henderson. Boston went

on to win the game in 11 innings and took the next 2 games as well, moving on to the World Series as the Angels went home brokenhearted. As they flew back after the final game, owner Gene Autry addressed his players with the best movie-star smile he could muster. "Look, you did your best," he said. "Your best on this day wasn't good enough." It would be a long time before the Angels would see the postseason again.

After suffering losing seasons in both 1987, when Joyner broke out with 34 homers, and 1988, the 1989 Angels recaptured some of their swagger. Newly acquired curveball pitcher Bert Blyleven led the team with 17 wins, just ahead of Chuck Finley's 16 victories. Along with reliever Bryan Harvey, who picked up 25 saves for the Angels, they kept California in contention for most of the season. Then a six-game losing streak in late September stalled the Angels' momentum and knocked them out of the playoff chase.

The Angels hung close to the .500 mark in the early 1990s but still found themselves left out of the postseason during the first few seasons of the decade. Even Finley, who recorded 18 wins in both 1990 and 1991,

Bert Blyleven was a well-traveled star, changing teams five times during his big-league career. Even though California was his final stop, he still had something left, winning 17 games and throwing a league-high 5 shutouts in 1989 at age 38.

SHORTSTOP · JIM FREGOSI

Nineteen-year-old Jim Fregosi joined the Angels in 1961 and became the team's first star. The power-hitting shortstop compiled more than 1,400 hits and hit for the cycle (getting a single, double, triple, and homer in the same game) twice during his time in California. Although he was traded to the Mets for pitcher Nolan Ryan in 1971, Fregosi returned as manager in 1978 and led the Angels to their first division title. He left the Angels' staff in 1981, but Fregosi's managerial career continued until 2000, when he won his 1,000th career game with the Toronto Blue Jays.

JIM FREGOSI
SHORTSTOP

LOS ANGELES ANGELS

STATS

Angels seasons: 1961–71 (as player), 1978–81 (as manager)

Height: 6-foot-1

Weight: 190

- **6-time All-Star**

- **1,726 career hits**

- **706 career RBI**

- **Uniform number (11) retired by Angels**

couldn't get the team back to the playoffs. Then, buoyed by the powerful bats of shortstop Gary DiSarcina, right fielder Tim Salmon, and center fielder Jim Edmonds, California battled back into contention during a strike-shortened 1994 season.

In 1995, California got off to a swift start and maintained a winning record throughout most of the season. Edmonds and Salmon were assisted by rookie right fielder Garret Anderson, who won AL Player of the Month honors with a .410 batting average in July. By the time August rolled around, the Angels had a commanding 11-game lead in the AL West.

Then came one of the most memorable—and devastating—collapses in team history. California ended August with a nine-game losing streak and repeated that woeful feat in the middle of September. When the regular season came to an end on October 1, California had lost its lead and was tied for first place with the Seattle Mariners, forcing a one-game playoff. An incredible pitching performance by ace Randy Johnson gave the Mariners the win and squashed the Angels' postseason hopes. "We were the best team for three months," DiSarcina lamented afterwards. "But you've got to be the best team when it counts."

LEFT FIELDER · BRIAN DOWNING

Nobody worked harder than Brian Downing. In an era when ballplayers rarely lifted weights, Downing pumped enough iron to transform himself from a scrawny catcher to an All-Star slugger and near-perfect fielder. In 1978, he set a team record for catchers with a .993 fielding percentage; then, between 1981 and 1983, after he had moved to the outfield, he set an AL record with a streak of 244 errorless games. This stretch included 330 errorless chances in 1982, also an AL record, which helped earn him a spot on the Angels' All-Time Team in 1986, as well as a place in the Angels' Hall of Fame in 2009.

BRIAN DOWNING
LEFT FIELDER

LOS ANGELES
ANGELS

STATS

Angels seasons: 1978–90

Height: 5-foot-10

Weight: 170

- **.267 career BA**

- **275 career HR**

- **2,099 career hits**

- **1,073 career RBI**

MONKEY BUSINESS

It might have been Troy Glaus's power, Garret Anderson's consistency, or Troy Percival's late-inning dominance. Or it might have been the miracle of the monkey that propelled the Anaheim Angels to a world championship in 2002. The Rally Monkey made its first appearance on June 6, when the Angels were losing to the San Francisco Giants at home. The stadium's video crew attempted to rouse the crowd with a clip of a dancing monkey from the movie *Ace Ventura, Pet Detective.* Not only did the fans respond, but the team did, too: in the ninth inning, the Angels scored two runs to win the game. Thinking it might be a good-luck charm, the team decided to hire a monkey of its own: Katie, a white-haired capuchin monkey who had already garnered attention for her role in the television sitcom *Friends.* Katie became the star of a series of Rally Monkey film clips, including the popular "Jump Around" and "Believe in the Power of the Rally Monkey." She also became one of the stars of the season, having her most potent effect in Game 6 of the World Series between the Angels and Giants, when she helped the team rally in the seventh and eighth innings to force a series-clinching Game 7.

Although Troy Glaus mainly earned his pay with slugging power, he also showed surprising speed on the base paths, swiping 14 bags in 2000.

TROY GLAUS

ANGELS TAKE FLIGHT

To sharpen their edge, the Angels experimented with a series of changes during the next few years. First, they brought up speedy first baseman Darin Erstad, who stole 23 bases and scored 99 runs in 1997. Then they replaced manager Marcel Lachemann with Terry Collins, changed their name to the Anaheim Angels, and, in 1998, moved back into their newly remodeled home stadium, then known as Edison International Field of Anaheim. As their roster of young players matured, and the pitching staff flourished behind the dominance of intimidating save artist Troy Percival, the Angels started to pick up speed.

The final pieces of the puzzle came together under new manager Mike Scioscia, a longtime catcher with the Los Angeles Dodgers who had ended his playing career in 1994. Scioscia led the Angels to a winning record in 2000. Young third baseman Troy Glaus, who had joined the team as a shy 21-year-old in 1998, had developed into a bona fide power hitter by this time, leading the league with 47 home runs in 2000 and slugging 41 more in 2001.

With Glaus's help, the Angels were about to become the best team in baseball—but first they would have to endure the worst start in team history. On April 23, 2002, Anaheim's record was 6–14, leaving it more than 10 games behind Seattle in the division standings. Then, shortstop David Eckstein hit grand slams in consecutive games, and the team pounded the Indians 21–2 in Cleveland. Suddenly, the Angels had a new spark. By the end of June, the team was only three and a half games out of the lead in the AL West.

As the season progressed, Anaheim and the Oakland Athletics fought for the top spot in the division. With outstanding pitching by Jarrod Washburn and rookie reliever Brendan Donnelly, the Angels seemed destined to overtake the "A's." But then Oakland got hot, winning 20 consecutive games and ultimately capturing the AL West. Still, Anaheim's 99–63 record was good enough to win the AL Wild Card, sending the team to the postseason for the first time in 16 years.

Rookie reliever Francisco Rodriguez, a September call-up from the

CENTER FIELDER · DARIN ERSTAD

A former punter for the University of Nebraska football team, Darin Erstad was selected by the Angels with the first overall pick of the 1995 amateur draft. He quickly became a star, batting .299 in his first full season and raising his average to .355 in the Angels' 2002 world championship season. His strength at the plate was matched by his hustle in the field. Erstad played almost flawless defense in both the outfield and infield, earning Gold Glove awards for his performances in center field and at first base— becoming the first major-leaguer to receive the award for both positions.

DARIN ERSTAD
CENTER FIELDER

LOS ANGELES
ANGELS

STATS

Angels seasons: 1996–2006

Height: 6-foot-2

Weight: 210

- **2-time All-Star**

- **3-time Gold Glove winner**

- **2000 AL leader in singles (170)**

- **699 career RBI**

minors, caught fire in the playoffs. With his help, Anaheim quickly dispatched the New York Yankees in the AL Division Series (ALDS), then moved on to face the Minnesota Twins in the ALCS. Up three games to one in Game 5, the Angels put on an impressive offensive display, scoring 10 times in the seventh inning to ensure both a 13–5 victory and a trip to the 2002 World Series.

The Angels faced the San Francisco Giants and star slugger Barry Bonds in an all-California World Series that went a nail-biting seven games. With the series on the line and the Angels trailing in Game 6, Glaus ripped a double that brought home both the tying and winning runs and forced a deciding Game 7. The next night, Anderson's third-inning, three-run double helped topple the Giants 4–1. After 42 frustrating years, the Angels had finally won a World Series. "These fans have been waiting a long, long time for this," Glaus said as he accepted the series MVP trophy. "And I know we're happy to be part of the team to bring it to them."

BARTOLO COLÓN

HAPPY HALOS

The elated Angels slumped to 77–85 in 2003, but they quickly returned to form in the years that followed. In both 2004 and 2005, Anaheim convincingly captured the AL West crown. Powering the team were such newcomers as right fielder Vladimir Guerrero, a dangerous slugger, and big pitcher Bartolo Colón, who won the 2005 Cy Young Award with a 21–8 record. But the Angels could not get back to the World Series, falling to the eventual world champions in the playoffs

ARTURO MORENO

A MAJOR FIRST FOR MINORITIES

The Angels' ownership has always been newsworthy, from Hollywood legend Gene Autry to entertainment and motion-picture giant the Walt Disney Company. In 2003, the corporation best known for its theme parks and animated movies sold the Angels to a Hispanic businessman named Arturo "Arte" Moreno, who had made his fortune in the advertising industry. When he paid $184 million for a majority interest in the Angels, Moreno became the first person of an ethnic minority to have a controlling stake in a major league baseball team. But that distinction meant little to Moreno, who said it had long been his dream to own a team. "I'm proud to be a Mexican-American," he said, "but as far as being the first minority, I think most of us are immigrants from some place, and I think we always try to do our best to be Americans." Moreno endeared himself to Angels fans by reducing ticket and concessions prices and by mingling with them in the stadium during games. "I want to create a fan environment here where people come to the park, have fun, and remember that, maybe for a lifetime," Moreno said.

RIGHT FIELDER · GARRET ANDERSON

Garret Anderson weighed 190 pounds when he joined the Angels as a 22-year-old rookie in 1994. During the next decade, Anderson not only filled out his frame but his statistics as well. Always known for his ability to hit for average (he holds the Angels team record for most career hits), he also developed into a feared power hitter, belting 35 home runs in 2000 and compiling 272 round-trippers throughout his time with the team. Despite his success, Anderson remained under the radar of most baseball fans nationwide until he and the Angels caught fire during the 2002 playoffs.

GARRET ANDERSON
RIGHT FIELDER

LOS ANGELES
ANGELS

STATS

Angels seasons: 1994–2008

Height: 6-foot-3

Weight: 225

• 3-time All-Star

• 2-time AL leader in doubles

• 287 career HR

• 2,529 career hits

ANGELS

MANAGER · MIKE SCIOSCIA

Although Mike Scioscia flirted with the idea of leaving baseball when his big-league playing career ended in 1992, the All-Star catcher couldn't break the baseball habit entirely. In 2000, he signed on as the Angels' 16th manager and has since become the best in team history. Not only is his .550 winning percentage second to none in franchise history, but he is also the only Angels skipper with a world championship ring. In 2002, Scioscia led his team to a World Series victory and was honored as the AL Manager of the Year for his efforts; he received the same award again in 2009.

STATS

Angels seasons as manager: 2000–present

Managerial record: 980–802

World Series championship: 2002

MIKE SCIOSCIA
MANAGER

LOS ANGELES
ANGELS

both seasons—the Boston Red Sox in the 2004 ALDS, and the Chicago White Sox in the 2005 ALCS.

Those postseason defeats, and the team's drop to second place in 2006, left the Halos hungry for more. With talents such as the flamethrowing Rodriguez and newly signed outfielder Gary Matthews Jr. in place, they believed they had the firepower to reach baseball's ultimate stage again. "We think we have the makings of a pretty good ballclub," Angels general manager Bill Stoneman said before the 2007 season started.

The team's performance in 2007 proved Stoneman right. Despite an early injury to third baseman Chone Figgins that kept the speedster sidelined for the better part of a month, the Angels quickly gained the lead in the division and never let it go. But the momentum that drove them to capture the AL West wasn't enough to overcome the surging Red Sox, their opponents in the ALDS. Boston swept the Angels in three games and went on to win its second World Series title in four years.

That disappointing finish just fueled the Angels' fire the following year. With 18 wins in the first month of the season and 57 before the midseason All-Star break, Los Angeles played with a sense of urgency throughout 2008. By September 10, the Angels had clinched their fourth division crown in five seasons, but even then, they refused to turn down the heat on their opponents. The Angels won 13 of their last 17 games and finished the season with 100 wins and 62 losses. It was their bad luck to once again draw the Red Sox in the ALDS. Although Los Angeles won one of the four games, the team found itself making another early exit from the postseason.

Los Angeles finally got revenge on its AL Eastern Division nemesis in 2009. After a season marred by the tragic loss of young pitcher Nick Adenhart and injuries to the team's top two pitchers—John Lackey and Ervin Santana—the Angels finally clinched the division title on September 28 and prepared to face Boston once again. This time, Los Angeles dominated, sweeping the Red Sox in a three-game series before heading to New York to face the Yankees in the ALCS. The Angels stretched the series to six games, but the Yankees prevailed and went on to win the world championship. "It's tough for our guys to get this far and not quite get to your final goal," Scioscia said. That sense of

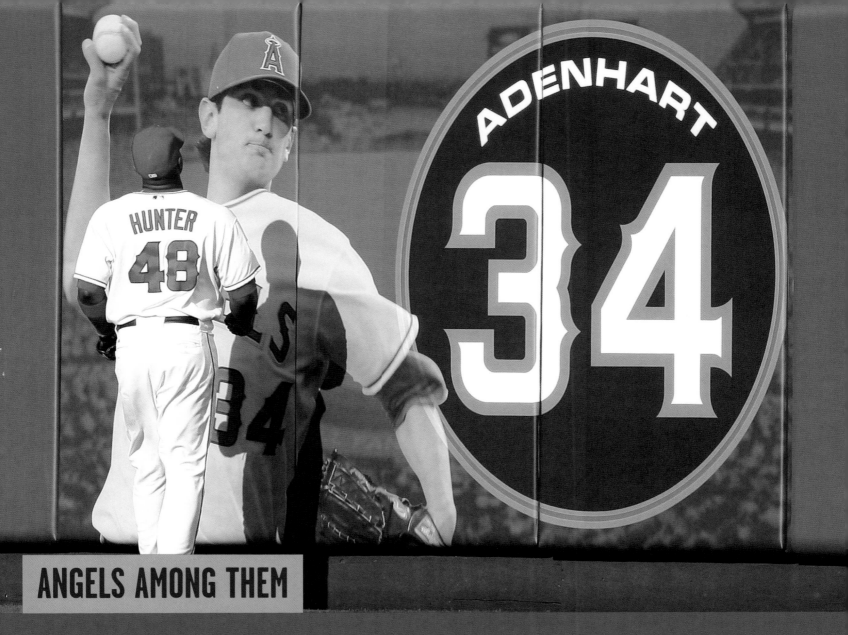

ANGELS AMONG THEM

On April 8, 2009, the Angels' 22-year-old Nick Adenhart pitched the best game of his young life, throwing 6 scoreless innings against the Oakland A's at Angel Stadium. But early the next morning, his career—and his life—was cut short when a drunk driver broadsided the car he was riding in, killing Adenhart and two of his friends. Adenhart's agent, Scott Boras, sobbed during a news conference later that day, saying that his client "felt like a major-leaguer" after finishing his start the night before. For the rest of the season, the Angels kept Adenhart's number 34 jersey hanging in his locker and carried it to the dugout during each of their home games. They installed a photo of him on the center field wall, which players often stopped to touch during games. And when the team clinched its third straight division title, Adenhart was included in the celebration, as teammates held his jersey aloft during the clubhouse party. "We wanted to celebrate with him like he was here," said reliever Kevin Jepsen. Adenhart's death was the latest in a string of Angels tragedies. Three players died in car accidents in the 1970s, outfielder Lyman Bostock was killed in a drive-by shooting in 1978, and reliever Donnie Moore committed suicide in 1989.

Howie Kendrick was among the AL's top offensive second basemen, swatting 41 doubles and driving in 75 runs during the 2010 season.

HOWIE KENDRICK

Workhorse pitcher Jered Weaver (below) and speedy shortstop Erick Aybar (opposite) helped make the Angels a perennial contender in the AL West.

JERED WEAVER

disappointment carried over into 2010, when—despite the slugging of first baseman Mike Napoli—the Angels sagged to 80–82, their first losing record in seven seasons.

The Angels have spent decades entertaining fans on the West Coast. Today, the star-studded team is more than entertaining—it is a perennial contender in the playoffs. As the Angels fly on, California fans in the greater Los Angeles area have every reason to believe their Halos will encircle another World Series trophy soon.

ERICK AYBAR

INDEX

Adenhart, Nick 42, 43

AL records 30

All-Star Game 9, 14, 23

Anaheim Stadium 10, 20, 24, 25

Anderson, Garret 29, 31, 36, 39

Angel Stadium of Anaheim 6

Autry, Gene 9, 12, 26, 38

Baseball Hall of Fame 8

batting championships 10

Baylor, Don 16, 19, 20, 25

Blyleven, Bert 26

Bostock, Lyman 43

Carew, Rod 16, 19, 20

Cerv, Bob 9

Chance, Dean 9

Collins, Terry 33

Colón, Bartolo 37

Cy Young Award 9, 37

DiSarcina, Gary 29

division championships 16, 20, 25, 28, 37, 41, 42, 43

Dodger Stadium 24

Donnelly, Brendan 34

Downing, Brian 19, 25, 30

Eckstein, David 34

Edison International Field of Anaheim 33

Edmonds, Jim 29

Erstad, Darin 33, 35

Figgins, Chone 41

Finley, Chuck 26, 29

Ford, Dan 16, 20

Fregosi, Jim 9, 15, 20, 28

Glaus, Troy 23, 31, 33, 34, 36

Gold Glove award 18, 35

Grba, Eli 9

Grich, Bobby 16, 18, 19, 20, 25

Guerrero, Vladimir 37

Harvey, Bryan 26

Jackson, Reggie 19, 22, 25

Jepsen, Kevin 43

John, Tommy 22

Johnson, Alex 10

Joyner, Wally 14, 25, 26

Kluszewski, Ted 9

Lachemann, Marcel 33

Lackey, John 42

Lynn, Fred 22

major-league records 8, 9

Manager of the Year award 13, 40

Matthews, Gary Jr. 41

Moore, Donnie 43

Moreno, Arturo "Arte" 38

MVP award 16, 20, 23, 36

Napoli, Mike 47

no-hitters 8, 15

Percival, Troy 31, 33

playoffs 16, 18, 19, 20, 22, 23, 25–26, 29, 34, 36, 37, 39, 41, 42

  AL Championship Series 16, 18, 19, 22, 25–26, 36, 41, 42

  AL Division Series 36, 41, 42

  Wild Card berth 34

Rally Monkey 31

retired numbers 28

Rodgers, Buck 13

Rodriguez, Francisco 34, 36, 41

Ryan, Nolan 8, 15, 16, 19, 20, 28

Salmon, Tim 12, 29

Santana, Ervin 42

Scioscia, Mike 33, 40, 42

Stoneman, Bill 41

Sutton, Don 25

team name 10, 24, 33

team records 18, 30, 39, 40

Walt Disney Company 38

Washburn, Jarrod 34

Witt, Mike 22

  perfect game 22

world championships 12, 31, 35, 36, 40

World Series 12, 23, 31, 36

Wrigley Field 24